AIR FORCE

AIR COMMANDOS

BY NICK GORDON

BELLWETHER MEDIA • MINNEAPOLIS, MN

EPIC

EPIC BOOKS are no ordinary books. They burst with intense action, high-speed heroics, and shadows of the unknown. Are you ready for an Epic adventure?

This edition first published in 2013 by Bellwether Media, Inc.

Library of Congress Cataloging-in-Publication Data

Gordon, Nick.
Air Force Air Commandos / by Nick Gordon.
p. cm. – (Epic: U.S. Military)
Includes bibliographical references and index.
Summary: "Engaging images accompany information about Air Force Air Commandos. The combination of high-interest subject matter and light text is intended for students in grades 2 through 7"–Provided by publisher.
Audience: Grades 2-7.
ISBN 978-1-60014-873-6 (hbk. : alk. paper)
1. United States. Air Force–Commando troops–Juvenile literature. I. Title.
UG633.G626 2013
356'.167–dc23

2012032063

Printed in the United States of America, North Mankato, MN.

The photographs in this book are reproduced through the courtesy of the United States Department of Defense. A special thanks to Romeo Gacad/AFP/Newscom for contributing the photo on p. 9 (right).

TABLE OF CONTENTS

AIR FORCE AIR COMMANDOS

Air commandos are **elite** members of the United States Air Force. They carry out secret **missions** for the Air Force Special Operations Command.

Air commandos train at the U.S. Air Force Special Operations School in Florida. They prepare for extreme ground combat.

AIR COMMANDO FACT

Air commandos in training are called swamp rats.

AIR FORCE AIR COMMANDOS

Founded:	**1944**
Headquarters:	**Hurlburt Field, Florida**
Motto:	**"Any Time, Any Place"**
Size:	**More than 8,000 personnel**
Major Engagements:	**Gulf War, Afghanistan War, Iraq War, War on Terror**

AIR COMMANDO VEHICLES AND GEAR

Air commandos fly into battle in the CV-22 Osprey and other aircraft. **All-Terrain Vehicles (ATVs)** are used for ground transport.

CV-22 OSPREY
06
ATV

Night-vision goggles allow air commandos to see in the dark. The **Global Positioning System (GPS)** helps them find targets.

AIR COMMANDO FACT

Air commandos can order airstrikes. U.S. planes then drop bombs on enemy bases and weapons.

Air commandos carry guns into combat. They use M9 pistols. Larger guns include the Squad Automatic Weapon and the M4 **carbine**.

M4 CARBINE

Air commandos sometimes need explosives. They may use **grenade launchers** or **rocket-propelled grenades**.

ROCKET-PROPELLED GRENADE

AIR COMMANDO MISSIONS

Air commandos perform several missions. They do **pararescue** to pull U.S. troops from danger. They parachute from aircraft during these missions.

Air commandos also **seize** and set up **airfields**. The U.S. Air Force uses the airfields as bases for planes and helicopters.

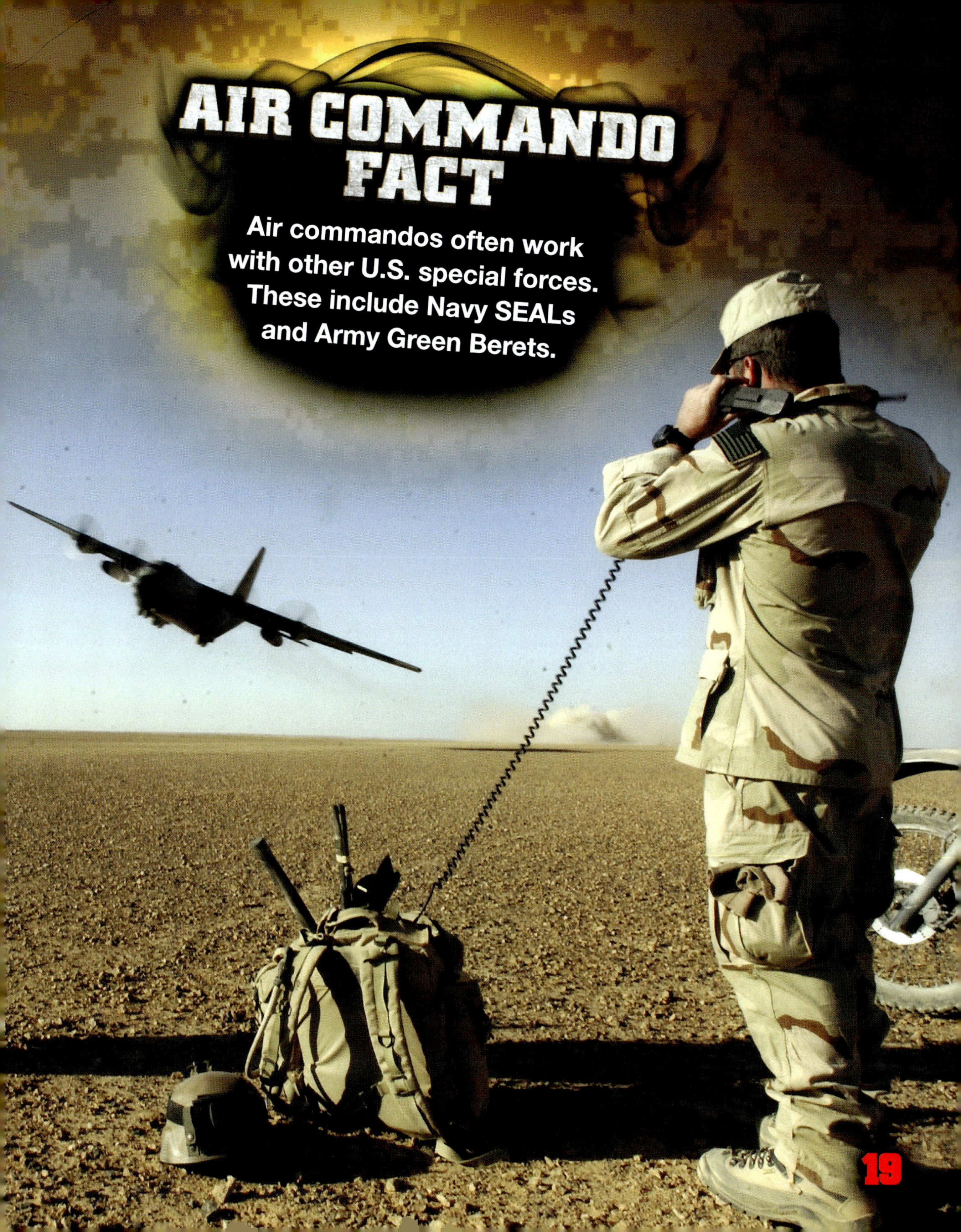

AIR COMMANDO FACT

Air commandos often work with other U.S. special forces. These include Navy SEALs and Army Green Berets.

The enemy can expect air commandos any place, any time. These highly trained warriors are always ready to rescue or attack.

GLOSSARY

airfields—places where aircraft can gather, take off, and land

All-Terrain Vehicles (ATVs)—small vehicles that can drive over any type of land

carbine—a lightweight rifle with a short barrel

elite—the most skilled

Global Positioning System (GPS)—a system that shows users exactly where they are on Earth; GPS also helps guide users to new locations.

grenade launchers—weapons that launch small explosives called grenades

missions—military tasks

night-vision goggles—special glasses that allow the wearer to see in the dark

pararescue—a mission in which air commandos parachute from an aircraft to find and rescue troops in enemy or hard-to-reach territory

rocket-propelled grenades—shoulder-mounted weapons that fire rockets carrying small explosives called grenades

seize—to take something by force

TO LEARN MORE

At the Library

David, Jack. *Air Force Air Commandos*. Minneapolis, Minn.: Bellwether Media, 2009.

Gordon, Nick. *U.S. Air Force*. Minneapolis, Minn.: Bellwether Media, 2013.

Sandler, Michael. *Pararescuemen in Action*. New York, N.Y.: Bearport Pub., 2008.

On the Web

Learning more about Air Force Air Commandos is as easy as 1, 2, 3.

1. Go to www.factsurfer.com.

2. Enter "Air Force Air Commandos" into the search box.

3. Click the "Surf" button and you will see a list of related Web sites.

With factsurfer.com, finding more information is just a click away.

INDEX